PUNCTUATE IT!

PARENTHESES AND ELLIPSES

BY KATE RIGGS
ILLUSTRATED BY RANDALL ENOS

D1319172

CREATIVE EDUCATION • CREATIVE PAPERBACKS

Published by Creative Education and Creative Paperbacks
P.O. Box 227, Mankato, Minnesota 56002
Creative Education and Creative Paperbacks are
imprints of The Creative Company
www.thecreativecompany.us

Design and production by Liddy Walseth
Art direction by Rita Marshall
Printed in the United States of America

Illustrations by Randall Enos © 2016

Library of Congress Cataloging-in-Publication Data
Riggs, Kate.
Parentheses and Ellipses / by Kate Riggs; illustrated by Randall Enos.
p. cm. — (Punctuate it!)
Includes bibliographical references and index.
Summary: An illustrated guide to the punctuation marks known as
parentheses and ellipses, including descriptions and examples of how to
properly use them to denote extra information or pauses in thought.
ISBN 978-1-60818-735-5 (hardcover)
ISBN 978-1-62832-331-3 (pbk)
ISBN 978-1-56660-770-4 (eBook)
1. English language—Punctuation.

PE1450.R535 2016
428.2/3—dc23   2016002554

CCSS: L.1.2; L.2.2; L.3.1, 2, 3, 4, 5; L.4. 1, 2, 3, 4; RI.3.1, 2, 7, 8; RI.4.2, 8

First Edition HC 9 8 7 6 5 4 3 2 1
First Edition PBK 9 8 7 6 5 4 3 2 1

TABLE OF CONTENTS

INTRODUCTION

THE HOUSE AT THE END OF THE STREET LOOKS CREEPY. YOUR FRIENDS THINK IT IS HAUNTED. (YOU DON'T THINK SO, THOUGH.) YOU TURN ON YOUR FLASHLIGHT ... AND SEE TWO BEADY EYES! EVERYONE ELSE RUNS. BUT YOU LOOK CLOSER. THEN YOU SEE A TAIL FLICK. IT'S JUST A BLACK CAT!

EXTRA, EXTRA!

*P*arentheses and ellipses are like extras in a play. They may not seem very important. But you need to have them around, just in case! Some **sentences** need these punctuation marks.

An ellipsis is a set of three dots. (Use the plural "ellipses" to talk about more than one set of three dots.) Sometimes a sentence trails off. Other times you want to show a pause in a thought or speech. You can use an ellipsis in both of these cases.

As he slowly opened the door, Landon's heart raced faster ...

The ellipsis above adds a feeling of **suspense**. We don't know what will happen next. An ellipsis in the middle of a sentence acts like a break in the action.

A face appeared at the window ... and then it was gone!

What if you used a comma instead of an ellipsis?

A face appeared at the window, and then it was gone!

That would be correct. A comma comes before a **coordinating conjunction** to join two complete thoughts. A comma also signals a pause. But it is not as dramatic as an ellipsis!

PUNCTUATION PRACTICE:

Look at the examples below. Where would you put an ellipsis to show a break or slow-down in the action?

1) Was that a curtain flapping or a ghost?

2) Annika tiptoed across the creaky floor, and Max followed her.

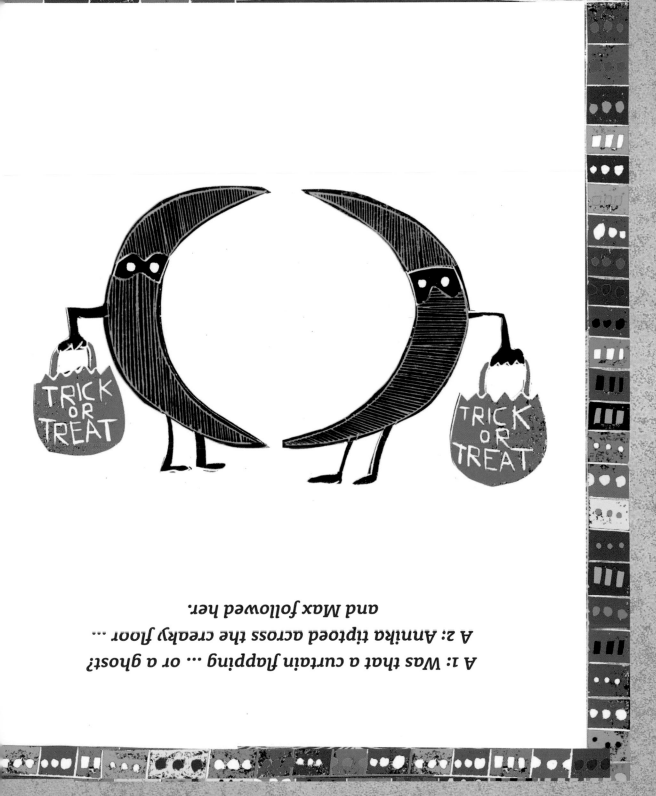

A 1: Was that a curtain flapping ... or a ghost?
A 2: Annika tiptoed across the creaky floor ...
and Max followed her.

WHAT IS LEFT

*E*llipses often show where words are left out. A direct quotation is enclosed by quotation marks. If you do not need to use all the words in the quotation, you put an ellipsis where the text was. Let's say your school paper ran a story about Halloween costumes. The following could be a direct quotation:

"This Halloween, everyone wants to be a vampire. Vampire costumes are flying off the shelves. Start carrying garlic now!"

You could shorten that quotation by using an ellipsis. Look for words that are not necessary to complete a thought. These words can be replaced by an ellipsis.

"This Halloween, ... vampire costumes are flying off the shelves." What you should *not* do is change the meaning of the original text. If you cut certain words from the previous example, you could be left with a completely different idea!

"Everyone wants to be a vampire.... Start carrying garlic now!"

PUNCTUATION PRACTICE:

Reread the paragraph after the quotation on page 14. How could you use an ellipsis to combine the second and third sentences?

A: Look for words that ... can be replaced by an ellipsis.

PUT IT IN PARENTHESES

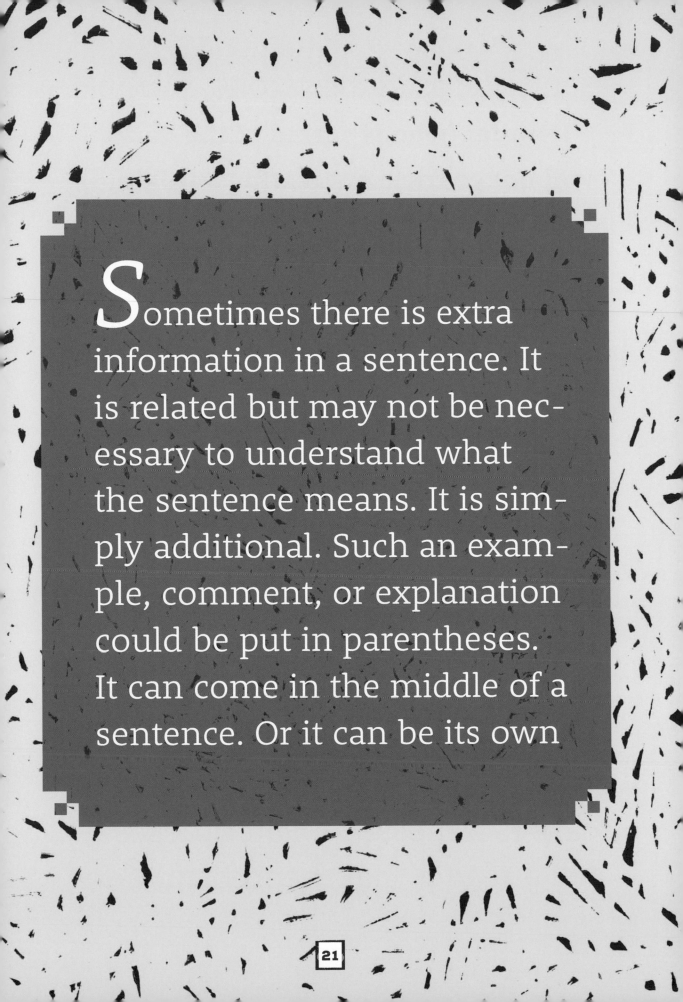

Sometimes there is extra information in a sentence. It is related but may not be necessary to understand what the sentence means. It is simply additional. Such an example, comment, or explanation could be put in parentheses. It can come in the middle of a sentence. Or it can be its own sentence, as in the second example.

Jennifer (who is scared of the dark) will not go trick-or-treating at night.

Vincent copied my costume idea. (I knew he would!)

When the extra words are within a sentence, they can often be written using commas or dashes instead. Take a look at the first example above. Now let's look at it with different punctuation:

Jennifer, who is scared of the dark, will not go trick-or-treating at night.

Jennifer—who is scared of the dark—will not go trick-or-treating at night.

The punctuation you choose carries a message! Parentheses tell a reader that the information is not very important. Commas tie the words closer into the sentence. Dashes break things up and create longer pauses.

PUNCTUATION PRACTICE:

Other punctuation can get tricky around parentheses. Here are some rules to remember:

- Do not use commas in addition to parentheses.

- A comma may follow parentheses in a compound sentence. (This happens when the two parts of a sentence are complete thoughts.)

- When a complete sentence is inside parentheses, use end punctuation inside the parentheses.

DRAMATIC STUDIES

Who knew punctuation marks could be so dramatic? Parentheses and ellipses are not necessary to complete every sentence. However, using them correctly (or incorrectly) could make or break the meaning of one! Keep these extras on standby ... and make your writing come alive!

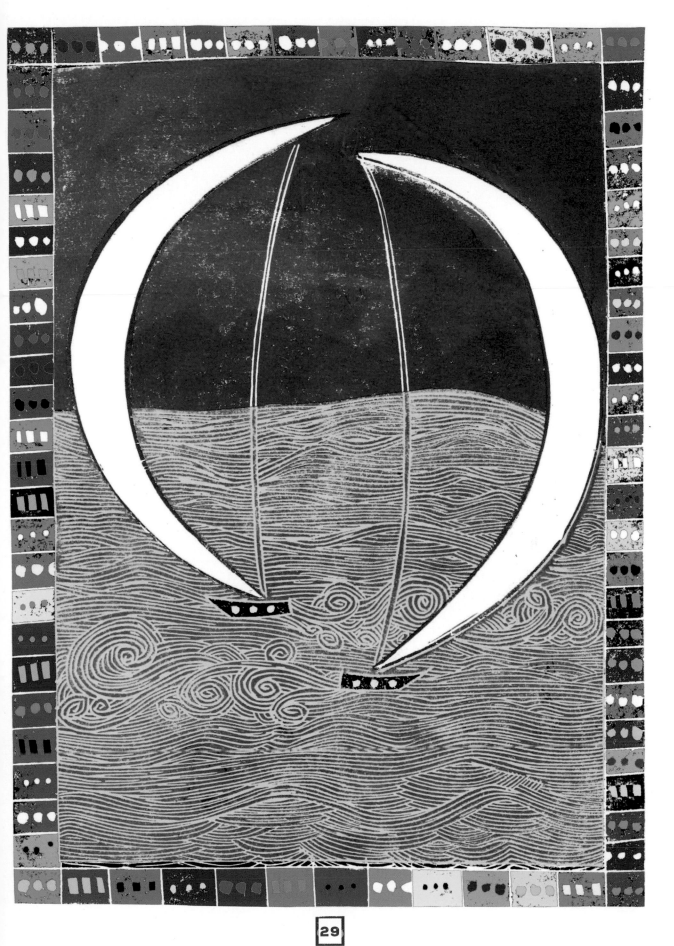

WHAT'S MISSING?

An ellipsis shows when words have been left out. In the verse below, some of the words to the song "America" are missing. Fill in the missing two lines.

My country, 'tis of thee, ...

_____

Of thee I sing.

Land where my fathers died! ...

_____

From ev'ry mountainside,

Let freedom ring!

A: Sweet land of liberty,
Land of the Pilgrims' pride!

GLOSSARY

coordinating conjunction: one of the words (*for, and, nor, but, or, yet, so*) that connects clauses

sentences: groups of words that have a noun as the subject and a verb

suspense: not being sure what will happen

READ MORE

Bruno, Elsa Knight. *Punctuation Celebration*. New York: Henry Holt, 2009.

Pulver, Robin. *Punctuation Takes a Vacation*. New York: Holiday House, 2003.

WEBSITE

Grammar Blast

http://www.eduplace.com/kids/hme/k_5/grammar/

Test yourself on what you know about sentences and other punctuation.

Note: Every effort has been made to ensure that the website listed above is suitable for children, that it has educational value, and that it contains no inappropriate material. However, because of the nature of the Internet, it is impossible to guarantee that sites will remain active indefinitely or that their contents will not be altered.

INDEX